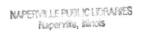

W9-CBR-134

PEOPLE WHO MADE HISTORY IN
ANCIENT EGYPT

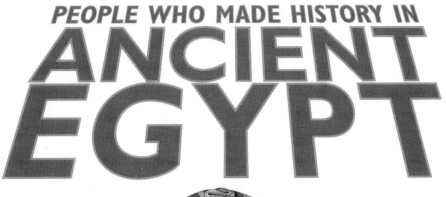

by Jane Shuter

Illustrated by Christa Hook

RAINTREE
STECK-VAUGHN
PUBLISHERS

A Harcourt Company

Austin   New York
www.steck-vaughn.com

Picture acknowledgments
The publisher would like to thank the following for their kind permission to use these pictures:
AKG Photo Library, London 24, 27, 28, 31, 36, 40; Axiom 10, 11, 14, 25, 32, 33, 34, 37; Dennis Day 5, 8/9, 12/13; Werner Forman 7, 9, 16, 17, 18, 19, 20, 22, 26, 29, 41; Robert Harding *cover* (background), 6, 30, 33 (bottom); Hodder Wayland Picture Library/©British Museum 38, 40, 42, 43/ ©Museum of Fine Arts, Houston 41

All artwork by Christa Hook except map artwork on page 4, which belongs to Hodder/Wayland Mapwork: Peter Bull

People who made history
Ancient Greece . Ancient Egypt . Ancient Rome . Native Americans

Published by Raintree Steck-Vaughn Publishers, an imprint of Steck-Vaughn Company

Library of Congress Cataloging-in-Publication Data
Shuter, Jane.
Ancient Egypt / Jane Shuter; illustrated by Christa Hook.
    p.   cm.—(People who made history)
    Includes bibliographical references and index.
    ISBN 0-7398-2748-0
    1. Egypt—History—To 640 A.D.—Biography—Juvenile literature.
    [1. Egypt—Civilization—To 332 B.C. 2. Egypt—Civilization—332 B.C.—638 A.D.]
    I. Hook, Christa, ill. II. Title. III. Series.
DT83 .S58   2000
932—dc21   00-036937

Printed in Italy. Bound in the United States.
1 2 3 4 5 6 7 8 9 0 05 04 03 02 01

Contents

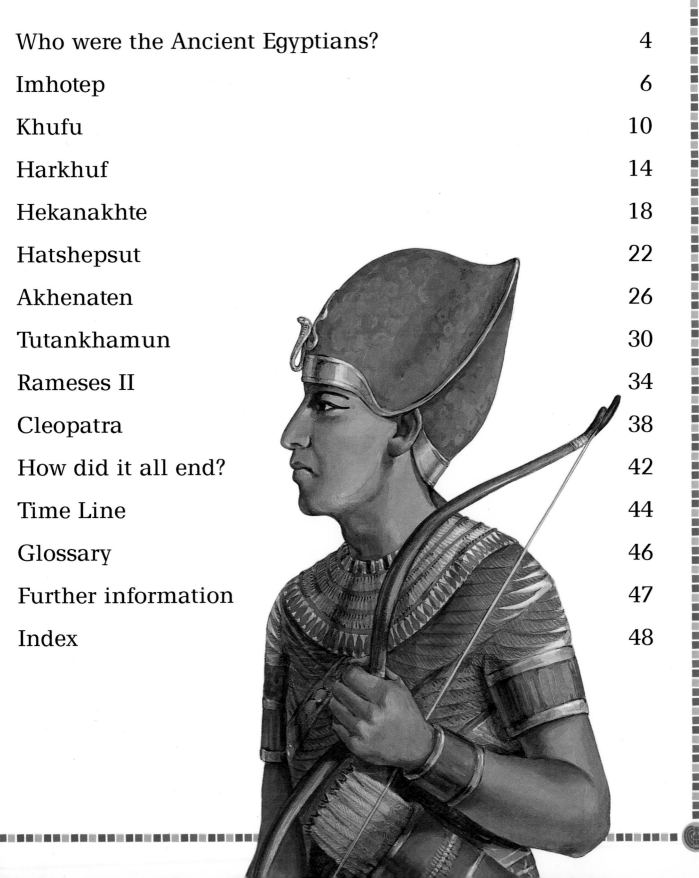

Who were the ancient Egyptians?

THE ANCIENT Egyptian civilization lasted nearly 3,000 years, from about 3100 B.C. to 30 B.C. It began when Upper and Lower Egypt were united and ruled by a pharaoh, or king, called Narmer. The people you will meet in this book come from different times in ancient Egypt's long history.

We know about life in ancient Egypt from studying things that have survived from the time. Little has survived from the time of the earliest pharaohs, so it is hard to find out anything about people, even the pharaohs themselves. Even the dates they ruled can only be approximate.

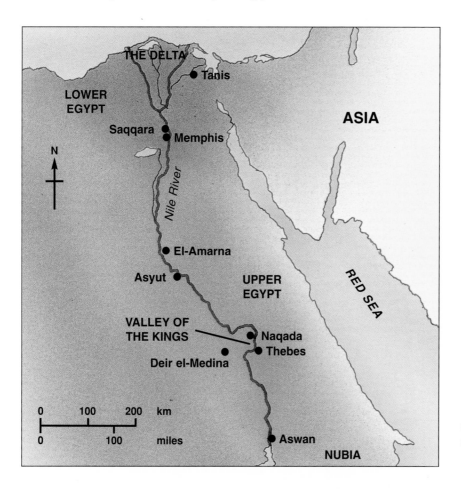

◄ Ancient Egypt was cut off by the desert and sea from easy contact with other countries.

Over 3,000 years, many things changed in ancient Egypt, but even more things stayed the same. One of the most important of these was that people lived in settlements strung out along the banks of the Nile River. The Nile flooded each year. This flooding was called the inundation. The thick rich mud the river left behind when it went down was the only soil fertile enough for growing crops. The Egyptians called the desert "the red land" and the fertile fields "the black land." The dividing line between the two was so clear that it was possible for a person to stand with a foot in each. It still is so today.

▲ The Nile as it is today. Water from the river keeps these date-palm trees growing. Water is carried from the river to the fields farther inland in a series of ditches —just as it was in ancient times.

It was vital to know how much the Nile was going to flood—that told the ancient Egyptians how much fertile soil there would be to grow the next year's crops. Steps going down to the river had markers on them, so people could chart how the river was rising.

A POEM ABOUT THE INUNDATION:

When the flooding is absent greed stalks the land,
Rich and poor alike wander the roads, homeless.
Yet when the river rises, sparkling, the land rejoices,
Every stomach will be filled.

Ancient Egypt in the time of Imhotep

BY THE time Imhotep was born, in the early years of the Old Kingdom (2686 to 2181 B.C.), Egypt had become one country, ruled by the pharaoh. Everyone, from the pharaoh to the servants, had a job to do. People did not change jobs, and most children learned to do the same work as their parents.

The pharaoh ruled from Memphis, sending orders along the Nile to the governors of different areas. These governors made sure that the orders were obeyed. For this to work, Egyptians needed to use a single language and to have people who could read and write it. These people were called scribes. The most important scribes helped to run the country. The least important scribes worked as record keepers—counting animals or checking grain into, and out of, the royal granaries.

◄ Scribes like this kept all the lists and records that made life in ancient Egypt run smoothly. They sat cross-legged, supporting their papyrus-paper scrolls on a board balanced on their knees.

IMHOTEP

**Scribe
circa 2675** B.C.

A FAMOUS SYMBOL

Pyramids were tombs for the pharaohs. Pyramids were built for some Old Kingdom pharaohs over a period of about 500 years. For most of the ancient Egyptian period, pharaohs were buried in other kinds of tombs, yet now the pyramids are among the most instantly recognizable symbols of ancient Egypt.

▲ Hieroglyphs were not written onto scrolls alone. These hieroglyphs have been carefully carved and painted on the inside of a coffin lid.

Imhotep worked for the pharaoh Djoser, who ruled from 2667 to 2648 B.C. He was Djoser's vizier, which meant he was the most important official and adviser. Imhotep was a scribe, so he collected and recorded important knowledge to pass on to other officials. He was a priest, as well as a royal adviser—in the Old Kingdom priests usually worked part-time. Scribes were often priests as well because both jobs involved reading and writing. Imhotep was also an astronomer and a respected doctor. But it is as an architect that he is best remembered because Imhotep probably designed the first pyramid.

◄ The young scribe Imhotep at work

SPOTLIGHT ON IMHOTEP

Name:	Imhotep
Lived:	Circa 2675 B.C.
Job:	Chief adviser, architect, doctor to the pharaoh
Family:	Father and grandfather builders and carpenters; we don't know if he had a family of his own
Interests:	Collecting and writing medical and other "instructional" writings
Features:	Like all ancient Egyptians, he shaved his head because of the heat, and wore a wig for parties and formal occasions
Personality:	Intelligent; not only did he know a lot, but he invented new building techniques
Special honor:	Being made a god some 2,000 years after his death

Imhotep designed the Step Pyramid at Saqqara. He is said to be one of the first people to figure out how to build in stone. Before this, homes, temples, and tombs were all built of bricks. The Step Pyramid set the pattern for later pyramids. The first smooth-sided pyramids were built the same way, then the "steps" were filled in with more stone.

▶ The Step Pyramid that Imhotep built for Djoser still stands at Saqqara.

EGYPTIAN MEDICINE

The ancient Egyptians used a combination of magic and practical herbal medicine to treat many diseases. Medicine was given to the patient and at the same time a spell was recited. The Egyptians thought both were needed for the treatment to be a success. If the patient did not get better, they thought the problem could be with the medicine or how the spell was recited.

▼ A statue of the scribe Amenhotep who lived 1,000 years later than Imhotep. Both were the only common men in ancient Egypt to be worshiped as gods after their lifetimes.

Imhotep designed the Step Pyramid almost accidentally. He began with a rectangular tomb, the kind already in use, called a mastaba. He built a wall around the mastaba and its other buildings, but this meant that it could not be seen from outside. So he set a series of smaller mastabas on top of the first, until it was 200 ft. (61 m) high—clearly visible from Memphis, the capital city.

For his skills and learning, Imhotep was widely admired both during his life and after his death. He was buried close to the pharaoh, a great honor. Hundreds of years later, respect for him was so great that people began to worship him as a god of learning and medicine. The ancient Greeks identified him with their god of healing, Asclepius.

Ancient Egypt in the time of Khufu

KHUFU WAS pharaoh from 2589 to 2566 B.C. At this time the religion of ancient Egypt became more organized. Now some gods and goddesses were worshiped all over Egypt as the most important gods. One of these was the sun god, who was worshiped in various places as Ra, Aten, Horakhty, Atum, and Khepri. Other gods, like Sobek the crocodile god, were only worshiped in some areas. Stone temples were built for the gods, and scribes acted as priests on a rota system, working one month out of every three.

The process of embalming was developed. Embalming involved drying out bodies and wrapping them in many yards of linen strips to preserve them. The embalmed bodies, mummies, were buried in more and more elaborate coffins, with more and more possessions. At this time only the bodies of the royal family or important officials were embalmed.

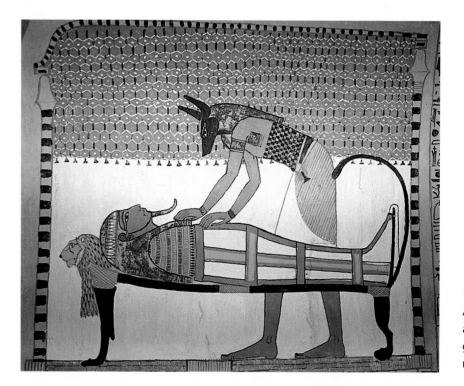

◄ A tomb painting showing Anubis, the jackal-headed god with an embalmed person. Anubis was god of the dead and appears in many embalming paintings.

KHUFU Pharaoh circa 2589 to 2566 B.C.

CRUEL KHUFU

Stories told many years after his death suggest that Khufu was a cruel leader. One story says that he had a man's head cut off to see if a magician who had come to the court could reattach it. He couldn't. Although these stories are entertaining, the chances are that they were completely made up.

▲ The furniture found in the tomb of Khufu's mother shows that craftsmen had a great deal of skill by this time.

Khufu—also known as Cheops— became pharaoh in 2589 B.C. and ruled for twenty-three years. Not much evidence survives from his rule, but we can guess at some things about him from what evidence there is. He was probably a strong ruler. During his reign the country was not attacked from outside. Instead, Egyptian soldiers kept tight control of the borders, especially the mining areas in the east, where turquoise stones were mined. The fact that the Great Pyramid, not begun until the start of Khufu's reign, was finished by the time he died shows that his control was tight!

► Khufu is wearing the red crown of Lower Egypt. The flail in his right hand is also a symbol of Lower Egypt and the cobra on the crown is a symbol of Wadjyt —the cobra-goddess of Lower Egypt.

SPOTLIGHT ON KHUFU

Name:	Khufu
Alias:	Cheops
Job:	Pharaoh
Ruled:	Circa 2589 to 2566 B.C.
Family:	Father was Snefru, the previous pharaoh. His mother was the daughter of an earlier family of pharaohs
Married:	Four times
Children:	Six sons (including the next two pharaohs, Djedefra and Khafra), three daughters
Personality:	Dutiful, but possibly cruel
Lasting achievement:	The Great Pyramid at Giza

Khufu was the first pharaoh to build a pyramid at Giza; earlier pharaohs had been buried at Saqqara or Dashur. Khufu's pyramid complex included temples as well as tombs of various royal officials and family members. He even had his mother's body moved from her tomb at Dashur, perhaps because it had been broken into, and reburied in a tomb close to his.

▶ The pyramids at Giza. The pyramid on the right is Khufu's Great Pyramid. The one in the middle, which looks bigger, was built by Khufu's son, Khafra. He built it on higher ground, so that it looked bigger than his father's pyramid!

In 450 B.C., over 2,000 years after Khufu's death, the Greek historian Herodotus visited Egypt. He saw the Great Pyramid. The priests there told him that Khufu had been a cruel tyrant, and that the pyramid had been built by 100,000 slaves. Herodotus was told the pyramid took twenty years to build, during which time all the temples were closed down, keeping people from practicing their religion.

We now know that the pyramids were actually built by ordinary workers, and that there were probably about 5,000 workers involved. From the workers' body remains, and from the hospitals and bakeries found on site, it is clear they were relatively well-cared for. It is also very unlikely that the temples were closed down. We know that common people were not allowed in temples anyway, only priests. How right the stories are about Khufu as a tyrant we cannot tell, but it certainly makes a better tale to tell tourists!

THE GREAT PYRAMID

The Great Pyramid had a square base with sides 755 ft. (230 m) long. It was made with more than 2.3 million stone blocks that weighed from 2.5 to 15 tons each. It was 479 ft. (146 m) high, and remained the tallest man-made structure in the world for well over 4,000 years.

IMHOTEPKHUFUHEKANAKHTEHATSHEPSUTAKHENATENTUTANKHAMUNRAMESESCLEOPATRA

Ancient Egypt in the time of Harkhuf

HARKHUF LIVED at the end of the Old Kingdom period. He was governor of Elephantine, modern Aswan, under the pharaohs Pepy I, Merenra, and Pepy II. Egypt seemed calm, but trouble was brewing. All through this period the gap between the pharaoh and important people, such as governors and priests at important temples, was closing. The pharaoh, who once ran Egypt and its religion alone, was losing power to these people. Raiders from the northeast began to cause trouble. Climate changes led to a run of poor crop-growing years, which led to starvation and discontent.

Pepy II ruled for 94 years. Toward the end of his reign he let local governors act more and more like rulers of their areas. When he died, there was no clear successor to rule after him. These two factors caused ancient Egypt to split apart for the first time in almost a thousand years. It took nearly 150 years to unite the country again.

◄ Governors of areas on the borders of Egypt often had troops of soldiers under their command, in case of attack. These soldiers are part of a model army from the tomb of a governor.

HARKHUF
Governor
circa 2300 to 2250 B.C.

GIFTS FROM OVERSEAS

Harkhuf brought back from his travels elephant tusks, panther skins, ebony wood, and incense. Harkhuf was not a trader. He went on his expeditions with a small army of soldiers and the things he brought back were described as "gifts." Some may have been given willingly, but some were taken by force.

▼ Harkhuf is shown carrying exotic cloth and ostrich feathers, brought back from one of his expeditions.

Harkhuf was governor of Elephantine. The city from which it was run was built at the point where the Nile becomes impassable for the first time. There were times when Egypt controlled the land far beyond it, and other times when these distant lands were overrun by invaders from the south. While Harkhuf was in charge, Egypt was firmly in control of the area around Elephantine.

From here Harkhuf led expeditions south, looking for exotic African treasures to bring back to the pharaoh. His tomb, in the cliffs near Elephantine at Qubbet el-Hawa, tells of these expeditions in words and pictures.

SPOTLIGHT ON HARKHUF

Name:	Harkhuf
Lived:	Circa 2300 to 2250 B.C.
Job:	Governor of Elephantine, had to keep the southern border of Egypt secure and lead expeditions into the south
Lifestyle:	Based at Elephantine, but moved around; needed to be prepared to organize the transportation of things, animals, and people back to Memphis
Family:	Came from an important family, trusted by the pharaohs
Personality:	Loyal, hardworking
Special honor:	Receiving a letter written by the pharaoh himself

Harkhuf's most successful "find" was made in about 2276 B.C. This was a pygmy who was a very skillful dancer. Pygmies from other lands were seen as special and unusual. They often became dancers or entertainers; few other jobs were possible. Egyptian-born dwarfs, however, could work as craftsmen, scribes, and priests. They could, and did, marry non-dwarfs and were not treated as unusual in any way.

◄ The ancient Egyptian god Bes was shown as a dwarf. He was supposed to scare off nightmares and other terrors—that is why his face is so fierce.

When news of the dancing pygmy reached the pharaoh, Pepy II (who was only about nine years old at the time), was so excited that he wrote Harkhuf a letter himself, telling him to take great care of the pygmy. Harkhuf got the pygmy safely back to Egypt and gave him to the pharaoh. The pharaoh was delighted. Harkhuf never again had such a great success.

A personal letter from the pharaoh was such a rare honor that Harkhuf had Pepy II's letter copied word for word onto the wall of his tomb, even the spelling mistakes! The hieroglyph for pygmy actually shows the pygmy in profile. Harkhuf died at some time during the reign of Pepy II and was buried in a tomb cut into the rock at Qubbet el-Hawa, overlooking the Nile at Elephantine.

▲ Harkhuf's expeditions would have been dangerous as well as exciting. When exploring unknown waters, it was important not to get stuck on sand banks. The sailor at the front of this model boat is lowering a weight to make sure the river ahead is deep enough.

LETTER FROM A PHARAOH

When he goes with you onto the ship, place guards around him, in case he falls into the water! Guard him while he sleeps and inspect him ten times a night. I wish to see this pygmy more than any of the other gifts you bring.

Ancient Egypt in the time of Hekanakhte

HEKANAKHTE WAS born in the reign of Mentuhotep II, the pharaoh who reunited Egypt and created a new capital city, Thebes, from which to rule. His rule began the Middle Kingdom period.

This was still a time of great uncertainty. No one was sure that the country would not break up again. Low inundations meant food shortages, and the country had not been united for long enough to build up emergency supplies of grain.

Farmers worked as they always had. After the waters of the inundation went down in late October, they plowed the land and planted crops. Water was trapped in lakes and channels between the fields, held back from the river with wooden barriers. March was harvest time. There was just time to grow another quick crop of beans or other vegetables before the flooding in July. While the land was flooded, farmers did other work.

◄ A tomb painting showing the tomb owner and his wife farming. You can clearly see the irrigation ditches that carry the water for the crops.

HEKANAKHTE

Scribe, priest, and landowner circa 1990 to 1940 B.C.

Hekanakhte was a scribe and a priest, who was sent north from Thebes in 1949 B.C., on temple business. The new pharaoh, Mentuhotep III, had been ruling for about eight years. While Hekanakhte was away, he wrote home to his family, and his letters have survived for us to read. They give us a fascinating glimpse of life in an ordinary ancient Egyptian family.

Hekanakhte wanted his farmlands well managed. He was afraid that his family might not stick to the ration limits that he set them. In times of poor inundations, when fertile land was scarce and food was short, everyone shared these worries. Low inundations tended to come for several years at a time, so all through its history ancient Egypt had periods of famine. It was one of the important duties of the pharaoh to make sure that the royal granaries were always full enough to feed his people in times of famine.

▲ One of the very few surviving Egyptian artifacts to show people as anything but well fed. It shows a beggar waiting for food to be given to him.

▶ A modern artist's view of Hekanakhte. There are no surviving pictures or statues of such an ordinary person. The artist had to imagine him from the tone of his letters.

SPOTLIGHT ON HEKANAKHTE

Name:	Hekanakhte
Lived:	Circa 1990 to 1940 B.C.
Family:	Mother, Ipi, was widowed and lived with the family.
Married:	Twice. Second wife, Iutenheb, bullied by the family
Sons:	Oldest to youngest: Merisu, ran things for Hekanakhte in his absence; Sahathor, carried letters between his father and the family; Sanebiut; Inpu, picked on by Merisu; Snefru, the spoiled youngest one
Daughters:	At least two, names unknown
Others in house:	A female relative, possibly a sister or an aunt; various servants, male and female

Although the letters give us a glimpse into the real lives of ancient Egyptians, they do not, like a story, tell us how things turned out. We do not know when Hekanakhte died or if his children ever stopped picking on his new wife, Iutenheb; or if Iutenheb ever had children of her own. These letters do give us an idea of how difficult it was for Egyptian farmers though.

▶ In ancient Egypt life was hard for farmers. This farmer is being beaten for not paying his taxes.

Extracts from Hekanakhte's letters

Look after all my property! You are responsible for it! Make sure Heti's son Nakht farms the 30 arouras of land we rent at Per-Haa; pay the rent with the cloth woven there. If you want to farm 20 arouras more then farm it! You'll find land—about 10 arouras for emmer and 10 for barley—to rent from Khepshyt. Don't use just anyone's land!

Pay Nakht one sack of barley for a month and 5 gallons of barley for his dependents extra. Look, if you give him more, I'll treat it as stealing.

Now what's the idea of sending me our old northern barley last time? So you will eat the good barley while I'm neglected? Now the boat's come home for you, I've caught you acting badly!

Make sure the servant Senen is thrown out of my house. You let her do evil against my new wife. Look, why must I nag you? What can she do against you, five children?

How are you, are you alive, prosperous, healthy? Don't worry about me, I'm alive. Look, I came down and fixed your rations. Now, the inundation isn't very high, is it? So keep to the list of rations below! Look, I've managed to keep you all alive up till now. Don't be angry about this. Being half alive is better than being dead altogether. You don't know real hunger—they are eating people up here.

1 aroura = about ⅔ of an acre, supposed to be able to grow enough to support one family. Many ordinary farmers just farmed 1 aroura, but they could farm up to 10. More important people could farm more land.

CLAIM TO FAME

Agatha Christie read translations of the letters, and based her detective novel *Death Comes As the End* on the people in them.

Ancient Egypt in the time of Hatshepsut

BY THE time Hatshepsut became pharaoh, ancient Egypt had passed out of the Middle Kingdom period, survived another period of break-up under several rulers, and reunited. This time is called the New Kingdom period. There had been nearly eighty years of peace when she took over.

The New Kingdom period has left archaeologists with the most surviving evidence of ancient Egypt. More and more people were embalmed and buried in tombs filled with furniture and other possessions, and painted with scenes of the afterlife. As the afterlife was supposed to be just like real life, but perfect, these things tell us a lot about everyday life at the time. Many of the ways of making pottery, furniture, metal objects, and jewelry were the same as in earlier times. But the objects were often more decorated. Furniture was made with glued joints for the first time. In Hatshepsut's reign, many new temples were built, especially to the god Amun.

▶ Paintings from the New Kingdom period were more detailed than before. These people look more natural than people on previous tomb paintings.

HATSHEPSUT
Pharaoh
circa 1480 B.C.

Hatshepsut was the daughter of the pharaoh Thutmose I. Her father had more than one wife, as was usual for pharaohs, and she was married to her half-brother Thutmose II. She had just one child, a daughter. Thutmose II had a son with another wife who became Thutmose III when his father died in 1479 B.C.

Thutmose III was still just a boy when he became pharaoh. Hatshepsut had been Thutmose II's chief wife so she, not the boy's mother, became regent. A regent rules a country for a child until the child is old enough to rule alone. For several years Hatshepsut was content to be regent. After all, she had the power, and she was making the decisions. But then, in 1473 B.C., she made herself pharaoh.

▼ Hatshepsut is shown with a crook, a symbol of Lower Egypt.

CROWNS

Pharaohs wore various crowns. The crown the artist has shown Hatshepsut wearing is the white crown of Upper Egypt. Pharaohs often wore this crown and the red crown (see page 11) to show that they ruled all of Egypt.

SPOTLIGHT ON HATSHEPSUT

Name:	Hatshepsut
Job:	Pharaoh
Ruled:	Circa 1473 to 1458 B.C.
Family:	Father was pharaoh Thutmose I, mother Ahmose Nefertari, sister of the previous pharaoh
Married:	Thutmose II, her half-brother
Children:	One daughter, Neferure
Coruler:	Regent for Thutmose III, son of her husband, Thutmose II, by another wife
Lasting achievement:	Her temple at Deir el-Bahri
Biggest failure:	Not to be remembered as pharaoh. Her reign as pharaoh was deleted from all stone monuments, temples, and tombs.

Hatshepsut dressed as a pharaoh and carvings from her rule often refer to her as "he." Despite the shock to the officials who ran Egypt, it is unclear how much ordinary people understood about what was going on. Her reign was peaceful; she even sent armies into other countries, something only strong pharaohs did.

► Hatshepsut had carvings of herself as pharaoh showing her with a male body and the symbols of male pharaohs. Here she is also wearing the male false beard that pharaohs wore.

We do not know why Hatshepsut decided to make herself pharaoh. It was a shock. While the ancient Egyptians did not think men were better than women, they saw men and women as different and expected them to do different jobs. Being regent was a job a woman could do.

When Thutmose III was old enough to rule, Hatshepsut vanished. There is no evidence about what happened to her. Perhaps she handed over power happily or maybe she was forced to. However, what is certain is that statues and carved references to her as pharaoh were removed, possibly some years later by Rameses II. Her body was not found in either the tomb prepared for her as queen, or the later tomb she had made for herself in the Valley of the Kings.

▲ The temples Hatshepsut had built as pharaoh were not destroyed—that would upset the gods. The carvings in the temple at Deir el-Bahri tell us how she made herself pharaoh.

TRADING WITH AFRICA

Hatshepsut was eager to show herself as a strong ruler. She wanted people to think that she could control other countries. Some of the carvings in her temple at Deir el-Bahri show a very successful trading trip to Punt in East Africa.

Ancient Egypt in the time of Akhenaten

AKHENATEN CAME to the throne after a long period of prosperity under New Kingdom pharaohs. Egypt had taken over more lands to the south and east, and had started to trade with new countries too. New technologies, such as glass-blowing, allowed craftsmen to make more and more beautiful jewelry, bowls, and containers.

Under Akhenaten there were religious changes. There were also changes in art. Earlier Egyptian painting had strict rules about how to draw people and what colors could be used. Under Akhenaten a new, more natural, style developed. People, things, and animals looked less stiff and much more lifelike. Pots, walls, jewelry, and furniture became much more complicated and decorated in a riot of color. Because Akhenaten moved the capital of Egypt from Thebes to el-Amarna, this new style is often called Amarna style.

▼ These ancient Egyptian glass containers are for makeup. Glass-making was a new skill, so these containers would have been expensive to buy.

AKHENATEN Pharaoh circa 1352 to 1336 B.C.

GODS AND GODDESSES

Believing in just one god is called monotheism. Most early peoples believed in many gods and goddesses, many of them connected with natural things, like the sun and the earth. Akhenaten is the first known follower of monotheism. Now most world religions are based on the teachings of a single person.

► This relief shows Akhenaten and his wife Nefertiti, worshiping Aten.

Akhenaten was the only pharaoh in ancient Egypt's long history to try to change the religion of the country. He could do this because pharaohs ran the country and the church. Instead of worshiping many different gods, he worshiped just one—Aten, the sun god. The sun god, who had various names and shapes, had been the most important god in the old religion. In the new religion he was the only god. He had one name, Aten, and one shape, the disk of the sun.

◄ Akhenaten was unusual for an ancient Egyptian, because he thought change was good.

27

SPOTLIGHT ON AKHENATEN

Name:	Akhenaten
Alias:	Amenophis IV
Job:	Pharaoh
Ruled:	Circa 1352 to 1336 B.C.
Family:	Father was pharaoh Amenophis III. Mother was Tiy, daughter of an important official
Married:	Nefertiti and at least one other wife, Kiya
Children:	Six daughters by Nefertiti, also the father of Smenkhkare and Tutankhaten (later called Tutankhamun) by another wife, Kiya
Most noteworthy act:	Changing Egyptian religion to the worship of a single god
Features:	From early statues he appeared to have an elongated skull, long jaw, thin neck, tubby stomach, thin arms, long fingers and toes, thick thighs

Akhenaten had a new capital city built—Akhentaten, now called el-Amarna. In some ways this seemed sensible. Memphis, the first capital, was in the north, in Lower Egypt. Thebes, the next capital, was in the south, in Upper Egypt. Akhentaten was in the middle, and made it easier to travel from the capital to any part of the country. But Akhenaten and his family moved into the palace at el-Amarna and never left it.

◄ This statuette shows Akhenaten and his wife Nefertiti in the new, more realistic Amarna style.

Akhenaten showed little interest in the rest of the country, or in keeping its borders safe. When this happened before, pharaohs had lost power to governors inside the kingdom and to rulers from outside. When Akhenaten died, after ruling for seventeen years, there was a real possibility that Egypt would break up. If it was not to do so, it needed a strong ruler and a definite change of policy.

Nefertiti was Akhenaten's chief wife. She advised him and took part in religious ceremonies at el-Amarna as an equal. She is often shown wearing a crown that no other queen before or after wore—a sign of her special importance to the pharaoh. She died before Akhenaten, and her tomb has never been found.

▼ This head of Nefertiti was discovered in the el-Amarna workshop of the sculptor Thutmose.

THE FACE OF NEFERTITI

This famous head of Nefertiti was found in the workshop of the sculptor, Thutmoses in el-Amarna. When everyone moved back to Thebes from el-Amarna Thutmoses left behind the things he would no longer be able to sell, including the head of the queen.

Ancient Egypt
in the time of Tutankhamun

TUTANKHATEN BECAME pharaoh almost immediately after Akhenaten died, because his older brother, the pharaoh Smenkhkare, also died. Now that it was important to have a strong ruler to hold the country together, the new pharaoh was a boy just nine years old. Tutankhaten's vizier and regent, Ay, acted swiftly to keep control.

Ay married Tutankhaten to Ankhesenpaaten, the third daughter of Akhenaten and Nefertiti. He moved the young couple back to the old royal palace at Thebes. He made sure they traveled to Memphis, too. He changed their names to Tutankhamun and Ankhesenamun—ending with the name of the god Amun, not Aten. He changed the religion of the country back to the worship of many gods. The temples to Aten were pulled down. General Horemheb and his army settled down the borders of Egypt in the same way that Ay and his officials settled down the country.

▼ The decoration on this box from Tutankhamun's tomb shows him fighting against the Hittites. However, it is unlikely that he ever went to war.

TUTANKHAMUN

Pharaoh
circa 1336 to 1329 B.C.

▲ The decoration on this chair back shows Tutankhamun and his wife, Ankhesenamun.

Tutankhamun ruled from 1336 to 1329 B.C., although the ruler was really Ay. There is no evidence to tell us if Tutankhamun approved of the change back to the old ways that Ay made, or how he felt about being married so young or moved from el-Amarna. We know so little about Tutankhamun because he died suddenly, just at the point when he might be expected to start ruling for himself.

Evidence from Tutankhamun's tomb suggests he was buried in haste. The tomb was too small for a pharaoh. Only one room, the room where his body lay, had decorated walls. Some of the treasures buried with him have his name carved over a previous name. The golden cases around the coffin were put together back to front. The doors meant to lead Tutankhamun into the afterlife opened instead into this one. Too much resin was added to the bandages during embalming. The resin leaked downward and glued Tutankhamun's mummy into its case.

◄ Tutankhamun as he would have looked as a pharaoh

WHOSE TOMB?

Who was the original owner of the tomb Tutankhamun was buried in? No one is certain, but some people think, from the position of the tomb, that it was the tomb Ay was preparing for himself. When Tutankhamun died, Ay could have had the king buried here because it was nearly completed and he had big ideas for his own future.

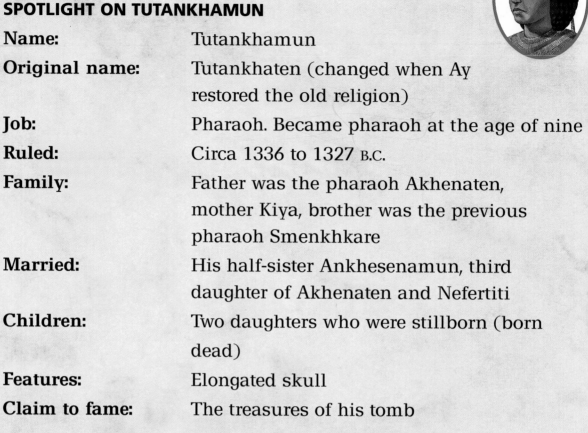

SPOTLIGHT ON TUTANKHAMUN

Name:	Tutankhamun
Original name:	Tutankhaten (changed when Ay restored the old religion)
Job:	Pharaoh. Became pharaoh at the age of nine
Ruled:	Circa 1336 to 1327 B.C.
Family:	Father was the pharaoh Akhenaten, mother Kiya, brother was the previous pharaoh Smenkhkare
Married:	His half-sister Ankhesenamun, third daughter of Akhenaten and Nefertiti
Children:	Two daughters who were stillborn (born dead)
Features:	Elongated skull
Claim to fame:	The treasures of his tomb

It is hard to tell for sure exactly how Tutankhamun died. Because of the hasty, careless embalming, archaeologists excavating the tomb damaged the mummy when moving it. It was so badly stuck to the case that they had to saw it in half to remove it. But the skull had been damaged in ancient times—it is likely that he died from a blow to the head. Whether this blow was the result of an accident or done on Ay's orders, we cannot tell. We do know that, as Tutankhamun died childless, the next pharaoh was Ay himself.

► The headdress belonging to Tutankhamun was found in his tomb. The cobra goddess of Lower Egypt and the vulture goddess of Upper Egypt show that Tutankhumun ruled both Upper and Lower Egypt.

CURSE OF THE PHARAOH?

Lord Carnaervon died, in Egypt, shortly after Tutankhamun's treasure was found. At the same time as he died, all the lights went out in Cairo and his dog, back in England, is said to have howled and died. The newspapers said his death was the revenge of Tutankhamun. In the next year, several people who had worked on the tomb died. The legend of the curse of the mummy had begun.

If Tutankhamun ruled only for six years and we know very little about him or his reign, why is he so famous? His is the only tomb of a pharaoh that was not completely robbed of its treasures by ancient Egyptian tomb robbers. His tomb was found and broken into twice, but each time the robbers seem to have been disturbed. The treasure they left behind included clothes, wigs, food, and wine, giving us a glimpse into how rich Egypt was at the time, and how skillful Egyptian craftsmen were.

▲▼ Just two of the smaller treasures from Tutankhamun's tomb. Above is a pendant and below is a board game.

Tutankhamun's tomb was the last pharaoh's tomb to be discovered in the Valley of the Kings. In 1914 the archaeologist Theodore Davis stopped excavating just a few feet away from the entrance to the tomb, saying there were no more tombs to be found! The tomb was discovered nine years later by the archaeologist Howard Carter, whose excavations were paid for by Lord Carnaervon.

Ancient Egypt in the time of Rameses II

Rameses II became pharaoh in 1279 B.C. There had been four pharaohs in quick succession in the 48 years since the death of Tutankhamun. Egypt needed a long rule by a strong pharaoh. Rameses provided this. He ruled for 66 years.

Rameses raised the biggest Egyptian army ever, about 20,000 soldiers, to keep Egypt's borders safe. He sent this army to fight the Hittites, to the northeast of the country, in modern-day Syria. The fighting eventually ended with neither side winning, but with the Hittites promising not to attack Egypt. Two of Rameses's wives were Hittite princesses, married to him as part of the peace treaty.

Under Rameses II huge numbers of people worked in stone quarries and on the sites of the many temples and monuments he had built. Some, but far from all, of these workers were slaves captured in battle.

◄ The beautifully carved and painted decorations on the walls of the tomb of Queen Nefertairi show the high level of craftsmanship under Rameses II.

RAMESES II
Pharaoh
circa 1279 to 1213 B.C.

From birth, Rameses was made very aware that, since his older brother had died, he was his family's only hope of keeping power in Egypt. As pharaoh, he had eight royal wives (two of them princesses from countries he had conquered) and many other lesser wives. Among them, they had more than a hundred children. Rameses II was leaving no doubt about there being a son to take over.

THE BIBLE

The Book of Exodus in the Bible tells how the Israelites, led by Moses, asked a pharaoh, thought to be Rameses II, for their freedom from slavery. He released them only after God sent ten plagues sweeping over Egypt. The last plague was the death of every first-born child, even the pharaoh's. As soon as the Israelites left, Ramses sent an army after them, which chased them as far as the Red Sea. God parted the sea for the Israelites to cross, then brought it crashing down on the Egyptian army.

►Rameses II is wearing the blue "war crown" that pharaohs wore in battle. He is carrying a bow. He would have fought by firing arrows from a horse-drawn war chariot, while the driver of the chariot also held a shield to protect them from enemy arrows and spears.

SPOTLIGHT ON RAMESES II

Name:	Rameses II
Alias:	Rameses the Great
Job:	Pharaoh
Ruled:	Circa 1279 to 1213 B.C.
Family:	Father was pharaoh Sety I
Married:	At least six wives, many more lesser wives
Children:	More than one hundred
Features:	Large, beaky nose; red hair. Lived to be more than ninety years old
Personality:	Determined. Good warrior
Interests:	Temple building, establishing the succession

Rameses II was, like his father, very eager to build temples and other monuments that would last after him. He finished temples his father had started, added to others, and built a giant mortuary temple for himself, the Ramesseum.

Rameses II lived to be over ninety years old. He outlived most of his children. It was his thirteenth son who finally became the next pharaoh, Merenptah. Many people say that the New Kingdom was never again as strong as under Rameses II. All the same, various royal families kept the country united for another 144 years; although for the last few, some governors were ruling almost on their own, as they had under Pepy II.

◄ This carving shows Rameses II as a young boy, ready to go hunting. You can tell he is young by looking at his hair. The single clump of hair is called "the sidelock of youth." All Egyptian children wore their hair this way.

▼ Giant statues of Rameses II from his temple at Abu Simbel. In the 1960s, the temple was threatened by the rising waters of the Aswan Dam. It was carefully taken down, moved, and reconstructed on higher ground.

FOREIGN RULERS

Each foreign ruler of Egypt treated the country in a different way. The Assyrians left local governors in charge, as long as the grain and other goods they wanted arrived regularly. The Persians, on the other hand, swept in to make changes, imposing Persian ways, including their own writing. This may explain why the next invaders, the Greeks, were happily accepted—anyone who drove out the Persians had to be a good thing.

In 1069 B.C. the country broke up again, at first into Upper and Lower Egypt, then into smaller kingdoms. Egypt was then taken over by Assyrians, Persians, and Greeks. Except for a sixty-year break during Persian rule, Egypt was part of wider empires, not an independent country.

Ancient Egypt in the time of Cleopatra

BY THE time Cleopatra became ruler, in 51 B.C., her family, the Ptolemys, had ruled Egypt for 251 years. They ruled as pharaohs, and built or rebuilt temples to the Egyptian gods. The Ptolemys came originally from Greece, but after Persian rule many Egyptians made Cleopatra's family welcome.

However, Egypt was still a conquered country. The official language was Greek, as were most officials who ran the country. The pharaohs ruled from the new capital, Alexandria, in the far north of Egypt on the edge of the Mediterranean. Egypt itself was rich and well run but Egyptian resentment of Greek control grew. Riots and rebellions broke out. The later Ptolemys, including Cleopatra, never felt completely safe, and relied on Roman help to keep power.

▼ The Rosetta Stone, written during the rule of the Ptolemies, has the same text in hieroglyphs, ordinary Egyptian writing, and Greek. Its discovery meant the hieroglyph code could be broken.

GREEK IDEAS

The library at Alexandria, set up by Ptolemy I, became a huge center of learning and culture. However, despite being in Egypt, it was spreading Greek ideas and culture, not Egyptian ones.

CLEOPATRA

Queen
51 to 30 B.C.

Cleopatra was the last ruler of Egypt. She was also the only one of the Ptolemys to learn the Egyptian language—all the others had just used Greek. She started her reign when she was just 19 years old. She ruled with her father, Ptolemy XII, for the last year of his life. Then she ruled with her brother, Ptolemy XIII, who was five years younger than she. In 48 B.C. she found he was plotting her death and fled to Syria, returning with an army to fight against him for the throne.

The Roman general, Julius Caesar, helped Cleopatra back to power, making her co-ruler with her younger brother. Cleopatra had a love affair with Caesar, and in 47 B.C. she had his son. In 46 B.C. she and her husband went to Rome to visit Caesar. They stayed until Caesar was assassinated two years later. They then returned to Egypt, where Cleopatra assassinated her brother and ruled with her young son, Caesarion.

▶ Cleopatra in the early years of her reign. Unlike Hatshepsut, Cleopatra never tried to rule as a pharaoh, so she dressed as a queen.

FAMOUS BEAUTY

"Her beauty was not of that incomparable kind ... but the charm of her presence was irresistible, and there was an attraction in her person and her talk ... that laid all who associated with her under its spell."

from Plutarch's description of Cleopatra, in his work *Mark Antony*

SPOTLIGHT ON CLEOPATRA

Name:	Cleopatra
Job:	Queen
Ruled:	51 to 30 B.C.
Family:	Father was pharaoh Ptolemy XII
Married:	Both her brothers (Ptolemy XIII and Ptolemy XIV) and Mark Antony
Children:	A son, Caesarion, who she said was the son of Julius Caesar and three children by Mark Antony
Personality:	Bossy, intelligent, ruthless
Most famous act:	Committing suicide when Octavian took over Egypt

Caesar was dead, but Cleopatra still needed Roman support. She met the Roman leader Mark Antony and persuaded him to visit Alexandria. By 37 B.C. they were married. This gave Cleopatra Roman support for her rule. Antony could use Egyptian money and supplies to keep his army going. However, Antony also married the sister of the man with whom he ruled the Roman Empire, Octavian. If Mark Antony had returned to Rome, treating his marriage to Cleopatra as a political alliance, he might have survived. He stayed in Egypt and handed over land that was part of the Roman Empire to Cleopatra.

◄ These coins show the head of Cleopatra. The ancient Egyptians only began to use coins during the rule of the Ptolemys. Before that most trading was done by barter.

▲ Julius Caesar, who helped Cleopatra become queen of Egypt and who was assassinated in 44 B.C.

Octavian convinced the Roman Senate that Mark Antony was under Cleopatra's control and no longer had the interests of Rome at heart. In 32 B.C. the Senate denounced Antony as an enemy of Rome and declared war on Cleopatra. In 31 B.C. Antony was defeated in a sea battle at Actium, partly because Cleopatra's fleet fled when they saw they were losing. When he saw Cleopatra's ships sail away, Antony deserted his men and followed.

By 30 B.C. Octavian had gathered a large army and was closing in on Alexandria. Antony committed suicide. Cleopatra met with Octavian, and tried to persuade him to support her. He refused. In desperation, she killed herself by getting a poisonous snake to bite her. Octavian then had her son, Caesarion, killed and made Egypt part of the Roman Empire.

A bracelet from the time in the shape of a two-headed snake. Cleopatra is supposed to have killed herself by letting a poisonous snake bite her.

◄ A portrait of Cleopatra wearing the vulture headdress of Upper Egypt

THE TRUTH ABOUT CLEOPATRA?

It was said that when Antony heard a report of Cleopatra's suicide he killed himself by falling on his sword. Cleopatra did commit suicide, but it was after Antony had killed himself. Some people suggest that she sent this message herself, knowing that he would kill himself when he heard it.

How did it all end?

THE ROMAN takeover meant Egypt was ruled from Rome. Egypt was no longer cut off from the rest of the world, and it was harder to keep foreign ideas and influences away. It was harder to believe that every other group of people were less important, less intelligent, or weaker than the Egyptians. While Roman governors and others who went to live in Egypt did follow some Egyptian ways, they also insisted that the Egyptians obey Roman laws and pay Roman taxes.

TOTAL CONTROL

The Romans ruled all of Egypt. But they settled mostly in the north of the country in Alexandria, the Delta region, and the Fayum. This area, once Lower Egypt, was more closely controlled. People in the hot, dry south of the country could break the rules more easily, as long as they did not revolt and as long as their taxes were paid on time.

◄ An Egyptian mummy from 2000 B.C. The Greeks and Romans were influenced by this ancient Egyptian method of burial.

The legacy

The ancient Egyptians still fascinate people today. The remaining temples and pyramids, built on such a grand scale and surviving for so long, are part of the attraction. The beautifully painted tombs and artifacts buried in them are another. But perhaps it is the mummies, actual people from the past, that draw most people to wonder what life was like for them when they were alive. Piecing together all that remains from the time helps us to build up a picture of real times and real people, like the ones you have met in this book.

◄ This ancient Egyptian jewelry is as beautiful as when it was made thousands of years ago by master craftsmen. Their use of gold and gems still inspires jewelry-makers of today.

SECRETS FROM THE PAST

The shifting desert sands still hold many ancient Egyptian secrets, even though archaeologists have been excavating there for over a century. As this book was being written, archaeologists who had been working for four years near the Bahariya Oasis, 185 miles (300 km) southwest of Cairo, found a graveyard that had at least 10,000 mummies in it. The graveyard was in use from 330 B.C. to A.D. 400.

Time Line

(Different Egyptologists use different dating systems to divide up ancient Egypt. The dating system here is the one used by the British Museum. Dates are approximate.)

Prehistory (250000 to 3100 B.C.)

250000	First settlements along the Nile River
12000	First archaeolgical evidence of farming along the Nile
3100	Upper and Lower Egypt united by the pharaoh Narmur

Old Kingdom (2686 to 2181 B.C.)

2667–2648	Djoser ruled
2650–2400	Great age of pyramid building
2589–2566	Khufu ruled
2530	Sphinx built
2300–2250	Harkhuf lived

First intermediate period (2181 to 2055 B.C.)

Different parts of Egypt were ruled by different kings and governors. Some of these groups fought among themselves.

1990	Hekanakhte born

Middle Kingdom (2055 to 1650 B.C.)

1940	Hekanakhte died
1880	Town of Kahun set up to build pyramid complex at Lahun

Second intermediate period (1650 to 1550 B.C.)

New Kingdom (1550 to 1069 B.C.)

Royals and important people buried in the Valley of the Kings.
Workmen lived in the town of Deir el-Medina.

1352–1336	Akhenaten ruled.
1350–1336	Tel el-Amarna flourished.
1336–1327	Tutankhamun ruled.
1279–1213	Ramses II ruled

Third intermediate period (1069 to 747 B.C.)

Late period (747 to 30 B.C.)

450	The Greek writer Herodotus visited Egypt
30	Egypt became part of the Roman Empire

Archaeological time line

1799	Rosetta Stone discovered
1816–1821	Belzoni started excavating in Egypt
1822	Champollion revealed the meaning of some hieroglyphs
1832	Champollion finished a hieroglyph word list and dictionary
1888–1889	Petrie began to excavate Lahun and Kahun
1894	Petrie began to work on "sequence dating"
1899	Petrie found the remains of the first royal mummy, Zer
1902–14	Davis excavated the Valley of the Kings
1922	Howard Carter discovered Tutankhamun's tomb
1984	Svante Pääbo cloned the DNA of an Egyptian mummy
1990	Richard Neave reconstructed the face of the Egyptian priest Natsuf Amun
1999	Bahariya mummies first reported

Glossary

afterlife   The place where the ancient Egyptians believed the dead went.

archaeologist   A person who looks for and studies things that have survived from the past.

architect   A person who designs a building.

artifact   An object that a person has made.

astronomer   A person who studies the way the stars move.

barter   To swap something you have for something you want.

capital   The main city in a country—where the ruler of the country usually lives.

climate   Weather conditions: temperature, wind, rainfall.

court   The pharaoh and the people who live and work with him.

desert   A dry place, having little or no rainfall all year round.

dwarf   A person of unusually or abnormally small size.

embalming   Preserving dead bodies from decay by making them into mummies.

expedition   A journey, often a long one, made for a particular reason.

famine   A time when there is not enough food, so people are hungry and sometimes die from lack of food.

fertile   Rich and full of nutrients —usually used when talking about soil.

grain   The fat edible seeds of some grasses. Barley, wheat, rice, oats, and rye are all grains.

granary   The place where grain is stored to keep it dry and to keep wild animals, like mice, from eating it.

impassable   Unable to be passed or traveled across.

inundation   The time when the Nile River floods each year and the fields are underwater.

mastaba   A tomb, dug into the ground, with a rectangular structure built over it.

mortuary   A temple at a burial place, where priests prayed for the dead and families could leave presents of food and other things for the dead.

official   A person chosen to work for the pharaoh. They made sure the pharaoh's orders were carried out.

pharaoh   A king of ancient Egypt.

priest   A person who worked in a temple, serving a god or goddess.

pygmy   One of a group of small people, who lived in northeast Africa.

Further information

regent	A person who rules for a pharaoh or king who is too young to rule for himself.
rota system	A system where people share a job with others and they each take turns to do the job.
scribes	The only people in ancient Egypt who could read and write. They did all the record-keeping.
settlements	Places where people settle down to live and build homes.
slaves	People who are treated by their owners as property. They can be bought and sold and are not free to leave.
successor	A person who takes over the position of someone who leaves or dies.
technology	The level of skill and machinery that people can use to make things.
temple	A home for a god or goddess where the god's image is cared for by priests and priestesses.
tomb	A place where someone is buried.
tyrant	An absolute ruler; someone who is cruel and hard.
vizier	The pharaoh's most important adviser.

Books to read

Crosher, Judith. *Ancient Egypt* (See Through History). New York: Viking Children's Books, 1993.

Harris, Geraldine. *Ancient Egypt* (Cultural Atlas For Young People). New York: Facts on File, 1990.

Hart, George. *Ancient Egypt* (Eyewitness). New York: Knopf Books for Young Readers, 1990.

Haslam, Andrew and Alexandra Parsons. *Ancient Egypt* (Make-it-Work! History). New York: World Books, Inc., 1995.

Marston, Elsa. *The Ancient Egyptians* (Cultures of the Past). Tarrytown, NY: Marshall Cavendish, 1996.

McNeill, Sarah and Sarah Howarth. *Ancient Egyptian People* (People and Places). Ridgefield, CT: Millbrook, 1997.

Nicholson, Robert and Claire Watts. *Ancient Egypt* (Journey into Civilization). New York: Chelsea House, 1994.

Websites

Also try general seaches on "ancient Egypt." New and different material is available all the time:

Ancient Egypt Webquest: http://users.massed.net/~mdirant/Ancient Egypt/webquest.htm

Julia Hayden's Ancient World Web: www.julen.net/aw/

Index

Figures in **bold** are illustrations